Changing London

DRAWINGS FROM THE PETERBOROUGH COLUMN OF The Daily Telegraph

COLLINS LONDON & GLASGOW

Changing London

DRAWINGS FROM
THE PETERBOROUGH COLUMN
OF 𝕿𝖍𝖊 𝕯𝖆𝖎𝖑𝖞 𝕿𝖊𝖑𝖊𝖌𝖗𝖆𝖕𝖍

by Geoffrey Fletcher

Printed in Great Britain by Wm. Collins Sons & Co. Ltd. London and Glasgow   SBN 00 410592 3.

Contents

Preface

Over the past 10 years some 400 drawings by Geoffrey Fletcher have appeared in the "Peterborough" column of *The Daily Telegraph* and readers often suggest their re-publication in a more lasting form. That demand is now partly met in this book, which contains 40 London subjects.

The reasons for such continuing popularity are pretty obvious. Any capable draughtsman can copy the evidence of his eyes but not many artists can combine, as Mr. Fletcher does, visual exactness with a sensitive choice of atmospheric detail. His hand does not merely record. It also comments, and in so personal a style that one does not need his signature to verify his work. It signs itself.

And it does so with passion. Mr. Fletcher loves London as Dr. Johnson did and, ideally, every inhabitant should. In 1777 his Scottish biographer Boswell suggested that if he too were to reside in London the exquisite zest of his occasional visits might "go off." To which Johnson gave his immortal retort: "No, Sir, when a man is tired of London he is tired of life. For there is in London all that life can afford."

There still is, of course. But less accessibly. Johnson's London was compact. His visits to the Thrales at Streatham made pleasant rural rides out of one of the most beautiful capitals on earth, its sky pierced by Wren's splendid churches, its streets adorned with the most refined domestic architecture ever known, its river a brisk and colourful highway on which, by the peculiar but stimulating custom of the period, one might amuse oneself with coarse raillery at the expense of others sailing past. Johnson was an expert practitioner himself. "Sir," he assured one who provoked him, "your wife, under pretence of keeping a bawdy-house, is a receiver of stolen goods." The word "pretence" is the mark of genius.

Alas, most of that vivid scene has long since vanished and the rest is being whittled away by commercial and municipal re-development tacitly aided by public and private torpor and neglect. This is what Mr. Fletcher, rightly, cannot endure and the process is more painful for him than for the generality of us because he knows London as few others do and understands better than most how grievous is this continuing massacre of fine old buildings—indeed entire neighbourhoods—and their human associations. A plaque saying "On this site stood . . ." when anyone bothers to fix it to some new and often inferior wall, is no more than the ghost of a ghost.

Some readers of the notes accompanying these 40 pictures may feel that Mr. Fletcher sometimes protests too much, that he should make a greater allowance for the inevitability of change. In fact, it would be an error to dub him a reactionary clinging stubbornly to objects doomed by decay or fresh modes of living. During his 10 Peterborough years he has often brought me studies of new buildings that have worthily followed old ones undoubtedly worth keeping but no longer fulfilling socially useful purposes. Change does not in itself offend him. He is a conservative in the true sense. His test is quality.

The quality, that is, of our whole ambience as well as of the materials, proportions and shapes of the buildings that individually provide it. The real reactionaries are those who hate all modern design and lump the good indiscriminately with the bad. Judgment of design is a matter of opinion, but there cannot be two opinions about what is happening to our background as a whole. It is deteriorating, largely through the pressures of population, traffic and noise, and will continue to do so unless public opinion nerves itself to protest as it did over the plan to engulf farms, fields and villages in a new airport at Stansted.

Greater London's population, now 7,900,000, has fallen by 700,000 since 1939 and the G L C think it may shrink by a further 900,000 in the next 12 years. That would mean more gobbling up for suburban houses of land we can ill spare even now, a serious reduction of the resident labour force and still further strain on the communications system. Already too many Londoners have ceased to be in any rewarding way citizens of no mean city. Most of them now live outside the region that furnishes a third of the capital's employment and their daily travel to and from it is an ever worsening ordeal.

But a town's function is to be lived in, not run away from or carved up by gigantic concrete highways. If the inhabitants desert—as for instance Americans are fleeing from the centre of Philadelphia to its fringe—the town's heart withers and for those compelled to remain living declines into a flat existence. Less explosively so far, this decay is also happening here. It is stupid, deadly and preventable and Mr. Fletcher is joined by all civilised Londoners in resisting it. For him and for them what matters is a right balance of new and old, present and past.

Readers of *Changing London* could begin advantageously by turning to his ninth illustration, of Georgian houses in St. Martin's Lane now replaced by an office block containing a cinema. He says the drawing best sums up the theme of this collection. We have seen the last not merely of a gracious 18th-century group but of the trimmings too. For the old gas lamps, modern electric standards have been substituted. These new shapes are often elegant. But that isn't the point. You can see them, or something very like, in every continent. Such uniformity is dull. The spice of life flourishes in its novelties, the things that don't exist wherever you go.

Mr. Fletcher's final subject is the charming 125-year-old sewer gas destructor lamp at the side of the Savoy. So many correspondents backed my 1968 plea for it that Westminster Corporation decided to preserve it as a curiosity. They were very wise; the curious is always entertaining. Yet the same body set about removing the equally attractive Art Nouveau lamps from Manchester Square for uniformity's sake and even the Ministry of Public Building, on the whole a reasonable department, was only prevented by public outcry from uprooting the interesting original lamps on Constitution Hill.

Such gratuitous acts, however minor they may seem in isolation, add up to a formidable drain of amenity which but for our Fletchers would be heavier still. These are not trivial matters. They imply ominously short-sighted states of mind. Take a stroll round some of the recent London developments, count the number of unlet shops and ask yourself why people no longer frequent certain thoroughfares that used to abound in bustle. The answer, I suggest, can be inferred from a sentence Sir Henry Wotton, the diplomat, author and Provost of Eton, wrote in the 17th century: "Well building hath three conditions—commoditie, firmnesse and delight."

We are not short nowadays of the first two. But delight is shrinking from our world and few modern architects seem to know the knack of it. Yet people have not ceased to demand it, whether deliberately or by instinct, and *Changing London* illustrates places that provide it. Or did. For this book has a historic value Mr. Fletcher will not be alone in wishing it lacked. Too much of what he draws has either gone or is going—some scenes unavoidably, others unnecessarily and to our shame. All to our loss.

Peterborough (F. J. Salfeld)

Introduction

Anyone over the age of three months could truthfully maintain that London was a more interesting and scenically satisfying city at the time of his or her appearance than it is now. It is as though London, in common with many other English cities, towns and even villages, were in the grip of a resistless, relentless malady, a craving for destruction, seemingly for the mere sake of it, like that possessed by the barbaric tribes which swept over Europe as the decrepit Roman Empire staggered to its end. Perhaps similarly the new barbarism foreshadows the advent of a new Dark Age.

But given the inertia, uxoriousness, corruption and the loss of will to govern that made the end of the Roman Empire inevitable, there was a certain salubrity, a purifying quality, latent in those destructions that only time could disclose. It seems a safe bet that the contemporary vandalism will have no beneficial effect whatever: all it will do is erase. Moreover, the present day vandalism is infinitely better equipped, organised and co-ordinated than the old one ever was. Not only does it utilise all the resources of modern technology, it also employs all the up-to-date techniques of persuasion and mass suggestion, for our new destroyers again differ from those of the Dark Ages in being a comparatively small minority imposing their will on the rest of us, fully conscious of what they are about, instead of the hydra-headed mobs of the Goths and Vandals.

But the result, to those who find their environment becoming steadily dehumanised and uninteresting, is precisely the same. It hardly matters whether one's home is destroyed to make way for yet another motorway or housing estate (and, curiously, I have never yet met any bureaucratic planner or private developer whose own home was ever in the way of progress) or burned down by some half-naked savage, unless, like certain modern theorists, one is able to accept nihility and decomposition as positive qualities. I can't, and the many thousands of *Daily Telegraph* readers of all ages who have written to me for the last decade can't either. With hardly an exception, the theme of the letters is always the same—anger, bewilderment, despair and a total rejection of the brainwashing explanations offered to them to account for the continual erosion of all that made London at once homely and magnificent, where the sense of continuity was strong, where the architecture was scaled to human proportions and where those things that satisfied the eye and fed the spirit could be found as much in the back alleys and humble terraces as in the precincts of St. Paul's.

In writing all this, I am, of course, expressing only my own convictions and not those of *The Daily Telegraph*. Such being the case, I am perhaps free to express another opinion of mine—that the old value and use of responsible newspapers in bringing these threats to light and making a stand for civilised values is the same as ever it was, unchanged and undiminished. It is a matter of some personal satisfaction that several of the causes espoused by the Peterborough column and illustrated by myself during the last ten years have had a successful issue: not many, it is true, in relation to the rest, but sufficient perhaps to justify one's existence, if human existence can ever be justified, which I am inclined to doubt.

A few of these victories have been included among the drawings republished in the following pages. I am aware that these and my remarks in this introduction will be a matter of mirthful impatience to all fully-fledged progressives, who think that history is bunk and architecture a machine for living in. Not that I mind. I don't believe that destructive changes—certainly not those I am here concerned with—are inevitable. I believe they are calculated and contrived, and can be accelerated, modified or entirely prevented, at will.

And I believe, with Ruskin, that the architecture we have inherited does not in fact belong to us or to any generation. It belongs to those who built it and to those who will come after us, ourselves being lease-holders merely, whose only task is to conserve and hand over. If this is so (and any other view surely implies that the passing moment is all important and all sufficient), I am at a loss to imagine what sort of account those of the mid-twentieth century will be able to give of their stewardship.

This knocking down of what our predecessors of the seventeenth, eighteenth or nineteenth centuries laboured to create and the erection of coarse, ill-proportioned or flashy substitutes, if not justified on the grounds of expediency, is normally described as "exciting" or by some other irrelevant adjective for the moment in vogue. I have even seen these tactics white-washed on the ludicrous ground that previous ages did the same thing, whenever it suited them, as Wren at Hampton Court, forgetting that in those days, when architects were also artists, their replacements were as good as, if not better than, the architecture they demolished. These melancholy reflections have been occasioned by my sifting through the drawings of over ten years, and finding to my surprise how much has vanished since the drawings were made. Though I find myself almost every week drawing one side of a building while the breakers are knocking down the other (as Ruskin said of himself in Venice) or preparing to do so, the full extent of the loss and the implications of it all can only be clearly grasped when records such as these are turned over. As time passes, we hear so many of these threats that custom familiarises us with them; the colossal staleness of the subject makes us unable to retain more than a vague notion of all that has gone or what will be the next to go; anger is blunted by repe-tition into lethargy and indifference.

It is difficult to believe that ten years ago there were no packing-case blocks surrounding St. Paul's, that, apart from gaps caused by war-time bombing, the whole length of Upper and Lower Thames Street was rich in interest—Gothic and Classic warehouses, gas lamps and the magnificent Coal Exchange. The Carter Lane area, as full of the minor architectural satisfactions of alleys and courtyards eloquent of the genuine old London town as any in the City, was not yet under threat of execution. London Bridge, perhaps with a judicious strengthening

13

of its piers, might have been expected by ordinary men and women to have another couple of centuries of useful life in it: now it is not only being knocked down, but it has also, if you please, been sold as a giant souvenir to the Americans. Once initiated, this contrivance of flogging our inheritance to foreign sentimentalists can be seen to have distinct possibilities—a new way to pay old debts, at the same time as we rid ourselves of lumber. Why not raffle off Dr. Johnson's house, export a round half dozen of the best Wren churches, do a package deal with some wealthy but architecturally impoverished republic for the sale of the Tower, complete with Yeoman of the Guard and printed instructions for carrying out its ceremonies? Seeing that we are intent on destroying Covent Garden, that unique blend of fine, curious and mediocre architecture, full of character and history, we could sell that, too, lock, stock and barrel, with a few hoarse market men, collectors of discarded fruit and old cabbages thrown in. . . .

Fortunately, the changes have not been entirely destructive. St. Michael Paternoster Royal, Whittington's church, has been saved from the threat of destruction, and restored. The lawyers of Gray's Inn, finding their ancient Holborn gateway to be very far gone, demonstrated their sense of civilised values by replacing it with a copy. The owners of Jack Straw's Castle, finding this also to need rebuilding, replaced it by a charming design, wonderfully loyal to the old weather-boarded village architecture of Hampstead, well-proportioned, full of right feeling and a credit to all concerned, though there were those who thought the new pub a reactionary pastiche, as might be expected.

A few of these changes on the positive side have been included among these drawings, as a sort of nosegay against the smell of rubble and brickdust, and to prove there are still enlightened councils, commercial firms and private individuals who know better than to allow London—or at least that part of it which is their concern—to become a mere money-making, soul-destroying machine, with a handful of selected sights, such as St. Paul's, left to satisfy the tourists. Bedford Square has in this decade been made the subject of a preservation order, and the cloud seems to have lifted from St. Pancras. These are two of the gains to be set off against a formidable list of losses. Ten years ago, when the mammoth blocks that contain in them nothing to satisfy reflection or thought, much less the imagination, were beginning to disrupt the London skyline, the London music hall, though at its last gasp, was still with us, with the Metropolitan in the Edgware Road still possessing a few years of life in front of it. Ten years ago, Euston Station still presented its old grimy front to Euston Square. The characteristic smell of the smoke of Derbyshire coal yet hung about St. Pancras Station, where steam locomotives continued to appear until about 1962. And so on.

But these considerations are too depressing, I feel, to dwell on overmuch. Meditations on what has been done to London and on what is to be done to it have an effect on the mind similar to that produced by the apocalyptic novel of Richard Jefferies, *After London*.

Therefore, a few words about the drawings themselves. Out of a large number published during the preceding decade, I have chosen what I hope is a representative selection, omitting those of temporary or parochial interest and choosing instead those of permanent and general consequence. The captions are the ones originally accompanying the drawings, re-edited and brought up to date where necessary and sometimes with my own comments subjoined. That this collection represents only a fraction of the modifications London has undergone during the period is surely an ominous symbol of the times.

Geoffrey Fletcher

1   St. Andrew's, Holborn Circus

DEMOLITION so often means the loss of a structure worth keeping that it is an unusual pleasure to praise what is happening at the corner of Holborn Circus and Shoe Lane. The drawing shows the demolition of Victorian office property and the consequent opening up of an attractive view of St. Andrew's Church, not seen for eighty years. The cleared site, which it no longer owns, is to be made into a garden.

St. Andrew's, commissioned by the citizens of London in 1686, is one of Wren's largest churches. It was gutted in 1941, and re-opened twenty years later after a two-year restoration. Since the drawing was first published, the site has been entirely cleared, disclosing once again the delightful figures of a charity boy and girl at the base of the tower.

St Andrews, Holborn Circus

2 The Leicester Galleries: Farewell, Leicester Square

THIS drawing was published in January, 1963, at the time when the firm was about to move to Mayfair. Since then, they have moved again, this time to Cork Street, and their former Gothic building has become a steak house.

The original caption read:

"After sixty years in Irving Street, the Leicester Galleries are preparing to move to Audley Square. They will keep their original name. The firm that presented the first one-man shows in England of Cézanne, Renoir, Monet, Matisse, Chagall, Epstein and Henry Moore has remained under the control of the Brown and Phillips families. When they move, a few years before the expiry of their lease, they will leave Leicester Square a legacy. They were responsible for the successful 'save the trees' campaign in the 1930s. Eventually the splendid late Victorian building seen in Geoffrey Fletcher's drawing can expect demolition. When that happens the site may regain its link with the arts. If the present plan to extend the National Gallery is carried out, a new National Portrait Gallery may spread there."

3　Box at The Lyric, Hammersmith

HAMMERSMITH has a plan to redevelop its King Street area which foreshadows the doom of a celebrated theatre. My drawing shows a box at The Lyric and some of the finest plasterwork in England.

The theatre was built as an opera house in 1890 and its great days were in the 1920s—*The Beggar's Opera*, etc. But for some years it has not paid. Now it is empty and the planners apparently do not think it would "work" among the flats, shops, offices and entertainments centre they envisage. I suggest they have another think. The Lyric, the most charming small theatre left in the Metropolis, is far too good to lose, especially as it is in a state of perfect preservation.

Detail of Box & plasterwork
The Lyric, Hammersmith

4 Eighteenth-century shop, Creek Road, Greenwich

T H E original caption read:
"Now, when a Greenwich antique shop is displaying, as a sad memorial, one of the eighteenth-century doorways from demolished King George Street, seems the moment to draw attention to this extremely fine late Georgian shop front in Creek Road, where several houses await the end. The drawing shows the superbly proportioned cornice and delicate Adamesque detailing which make it one of the few of this quality left in London. The shop is occupied by a second-hand dealer. If we cared enough about these things, steps would be taken at once to ensure the front's preservation—either in Greenwich or, better still, the Victoria and Albert Museum."

This story, however, had a happy ending. The fine double bow window shop front was removed without so much as a single pane of glass being broken. Eventually it will be on display in the new London Museum to be built at London Wall.

22

5 Albert Square, Vauxhall

UNDER the heading of *Once a garden, now a dump*, Peterborough rightly drew attention to the state of Albert Square, in Lambeth, near Kennington Oval, and remarked that "trees have been reduced to stumps, others are decaying and the place is a dump for old prams, mattresses and other junk. Yet the square is excellent mid-nineteenth-century stuff, and would look charming if cleaned up and replanted. And Lambeth is not so rich in open spaces that it can afford to let this one become derelict."

Today, Albert Square is less depressing, but it seems fairly safe to predict that it will never again recover the attractive appearance and genteel status that it had in common with other squares and terraces in this area in the 1840s.

24

6   Black Lion Yard, Whitechapel

ANOTHER stage in the process of wiping out London's traditional East End is reached with the impending demolition of Black Lion Yard, Whitechapel. The area was made notorious by the Jack the Ripper murders of the 1880s. My drawing shows the street looking south to the Whitechapel Bell Foundry, a centuries-old concern where Big Ben was cast, and, in more recent years, the bells of Washington Cathedral.

For generations East Enders have bought engagement and wedding rings in Black Lion Yard on Sundays. The alleyway includes a cowkeeper's yard, recalling the days when local dairies kept their milking animals on the premises. The cows departed long ago, but the shippons remain.

7 Silk mercer's shop, Spitalfields

T H E drawing and the following caption were first published in April, 1968:

"Six years ago I urged the conserving of the magnificent Roman Doric shop, originally a silk mercer's, which Abraham Swan designed in Artillery Lane, Spitalfields, about 1750. Now, with the aid of a Government grant, the owner, Mr. Stanley Moss, has had the restoration done by Ashby and Horner in conjunction with Szerelmey. My drawing shows the charming result.

"It is reassuring that not only the landlord but also the tenant, Marty Fashions, have been perceptive enough to care for this great rarity among London shops."

The door to the merchant's living quarters above appears on the right of the drawing. One of the features of this splendid shop is the quantity of fine Baroque carving with which its friezes are enriched.

8 Gothic off the Strand: Butterfield's Parsonage in Burleigh Street

A MORE cheerful story than the usual one of buildings being demolished for their site value is that a firm of architects has got the Westminster City Council's permission to convert into two flats the Victorian parsonage in Burleigh Street, off the Strand.

The red-brick, stone-dressed building is tall and narrow and displays an L-shaped front to the street. The site, restricted and sloping, was a difficult one to manage successfully, but the architect was equal to the task. It is a characteristic example of the original and stylish Gothic work of William Butterfield, who was architect of All Saints, Margaret Street, in Marylebone, and also of Keble College and the chapel of Balliol College, Oxford.

The house used to be the vicarage of St. Michael's Church, which stood at the corner of Burleigh Street and Exeter Street. But the parish was combined with that of St. Paul's, Covent Garden, in 1905.

Burleigh St Strand

9 Demolitions in St. Martin's Lane

THE first attack on "The Dials"—a district that had an inexhaustible attraction of horror for the young Charles Dickens—was in the middle of the last century, when New Oxford Street was driven through some of its worst rookeries and slums.

Recent development in the Seven Dials district has wiped out most of what remained, apart from one or two isolated spots, such as Shelton Street. The drawing on the opposite page was published at the time when this attractive group in St. Martin's Lane, the best of what had survived, was about to be demolished. At this time, Harrison's the printers, had sold their site there, and removed to Cavendish Square. Particularly good were the three houses on the right of the drawing. They dated from 1739. No. 43 (second from the right) was a fine example of Georgian town architecture, with pilasters and frieze and cornice in cut brick.

Today a modern office block containing a cinema occupies the site. Even the three old gas lamps in the alley separating this group from the back of the Coliseum have gone. Characterless modern electric standards have taken their place. This drawing seems to me to sum up the theme of this collection more graphically than any other.

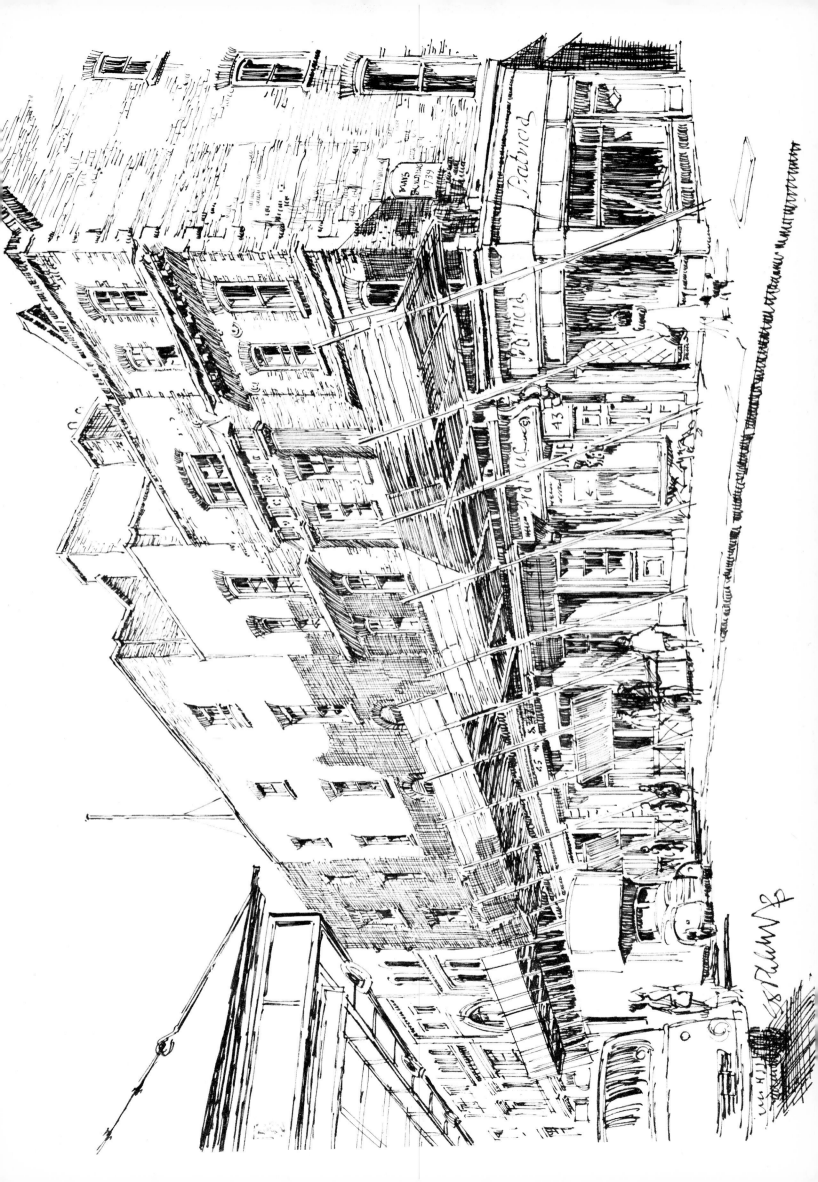

10 Kingstown Street, Chalk Farm

THIS drawing was published in July, 1968, with the following comment:

"North of Regent's Park a change of policy has come just in time for the houses shown on the right of my drawing. These nineteenth-century terraced cottages were condemned as slums, and about to be pulled down to make way for new development.

Most of the cottages on the other side of the street have already been demolished. But under a new policy, Camden Borough Council is to try to preserve as much as possible in such areas, which might otherwise be entirely rebuilt.

This is in line with the Government's White Paper *Old Houses into New Homes,* but whether it can be done throughout Camden remains to be seen. For the moment, Kingstown Street is safe, but it cannot be taken as more than a trial run."

Kingstown St
Hazel Park

Geoffrey McNully

11   A house in Cheyne Walk

"MY drawing of No. 37, Cheyne Walk, Chelsea," said Peterborough on September 7th, 1966, "involves a mystery. The house was designed and occupied by the Victorian architect, C. R. Ashbee, who also designed Nos. 38 and 39. It is as a group that these unique Art Nouveau houses are most interesting, and preservation orders have been put on 38 and 39. But the Ministry of Housing has refused one for 37, which is earlier (1894) than the others and possibly the best. No reason for this extraordinary inconsistency has been given, but the decision is thoroughly bad. If No. 37 were demolished and replaced the whole effect would be ruined—a point the G.L.C. has urged in vain."

As a footnote, it seems worthwhile adding that the subsequent demolitions from this corner eastwards to Oakley Street have been a severe loss to Chelsea. The destruction included the old pharmacy (later a grocer's) where Queen Victoria bought her scent, the memorable Blue Cockatoo (a restaurant which commenced business in 1914 and was found by the owner to be haunted by a female ghost), the Pier Hotel, Thurston's and the old smithy.

12 Victorian Police Station, Harrow Road

UNDER the heading *Blue Lamps for Old*, Peterborough published this drawing in 1963 with the following commentary:
"Paddington Police Station, the fortress-like Victorian Gothic headquarters of D. Division in Harrow Road, is coming down under a road widening scheme. As the drawing suggests, it will be no loss. It dates from 1865 and its entrance has the depressing quality of a Doré drawing. So has the surrounding district, the setting for the film *The Blue Lamp*."

For once, I venture to disagree. I love these frowning, intimidating Victorian police stations, and cannot bear the characterless, functional ones, such as those at Kingston, Albany Street and Theobalds Road, which are replacing them—barren designs only redeemed, in my opinion, by the re-use over their entrances of the fine Victorian lamps —old lamps for new, as it might be.

Such nineteenth-century police stations, of an indescribably mixed style, belong to the period of Charles Peace, dark lanterns and heavy moustaches. However, in view of the fact that today's bad lads have given up lugging bags labelled "Swag" and "Loot" and gone in for up-to-date techniques, we must expect their adversaries to do the same.

13 Westbourne Terrace

THE drawing opposite of Westbourne Terrace shows what can happen when a public authority lacks full control over a civilised scheme to save good architecture.

In view of a threat to one block, the L.C.C. made a preservation order on a large section of the terrace. But the Minister of Housing refused to confirm the order on the block. Thus the L.C.C. had to do the best they could to prevent the disruption of one of London's fine architectural vistas. After much negotiation, the developers proposed a new façade for the reconstructed block which at any rate came close to the effect of the original work.

14 Juniper Street

THIS drawing was published in 1966. The original paragraph, under the heading of *Unfragrant Juniper*, I transcribe exactly as it stood, for though demolition is going on all over the area, especially in Cable Street, generally speaking the comment still holds good.

"My drawing is a view of Juniper Street, in Stepney, near Shadwell Basin, which scarcely lives up to its name and which the G.L.C. want to clear and redevelop at a cost of £200,000.

"This region of tenements belongs to one of London's worst slum warrens. Some of the houses, though, have charm and would be worth restoring if only their surroundings were better.

"The building on the left of this sketch is an example. It stands at the corner of Juniper Street and King David Lane. The atmosphere hereabouts is Dickensian."

15 Burial ground of St. George's, Hanover Square, Bayswater Road

THE original paragraph read:

"Sir Keith Joseph now has before him an application from St. George's, Hanover Square, to 'develop' its old burial ground off Bayswater Road, near Marble Arch. To sell these five largely derelict acres would require a private Act of Parliament. The land was consecrated in 1765, closed for burials in 1854, laid out as gardens in 1914 and so badly damaged during the blitz that most of the graves are now unidentifiable.

"St. George's has no endowments and no money for the graveyard's upkeep. It contains two interesting tombs—that of Laurence Sterne, which may be moved to his Yorkshire parish of Coxwold, and that of Paul Sandby, seen in the foreground of the drawing. Sandby, one of the finest English watercolourists, deserves a better fate than to be dumped in some suburban cemetery. His memorial should be preserved."

The Parliamentary powers were granted. A planning application has been granted by the Westminster City Council for a private development of some 300 flats, on which work has now (January, 1969) been started.

16 St. Magnus the Martyr, Billingsgate

I ILLUSTRATE the good chance the City now has to compensate for the demolition of London Bridge.

"The drawing shows how Adelaide House was allowed in the 1920s to box in the finest of the late Wren churches, St. Magnus the Martyr in Lower Thames Street. Now the bridge reconstruction offers an opportunity to improve the view by opening it up.

"St. Magnus was built between 1676 and 1705, and escaped serious damage when the warehouse, whose ruins are seen on the left, was bombed. London Bridge's east footpath used to pass under the tower, and the church clock was the gift of a Lord Mayor who as an apprentice had been thrashed for late arrival at work. Miles Coverdale, who translated the Bible in 1535, was briefly Rector of St. Magnus, and is buried in the church."

The drawing was published in September, 1968.

17 John Loudon's house, Porchester Terrace

THIS pleasing late Regency building in Bayswater seems to deserve the preservation order which the Greater London Council tells me has now been placed on it. It is in fact a double villa—Nos. 3 and 5 Porchester Terrace—designed by the landscape gardener and writer, John Loudon. He used No. 3 as his home and office, and its garden was one of the most famous in London.

Loudon (1783-1843) was also a pioneer in wrought iron and glass construction, and originated ideas later used by Decimus Burton at Kew and Paxton at the Crystal Palace.

Loudon was also one of the first to recognise Ruskin's genius and the publisher of his earliest architectural writings.

A domed conservatory unites the two houses, and in front of them an Indian bean tree, probably planted by Loudon, still flourishes. Now they are to be preserved, the question of restoring the pair as a whole arises. No. 5's condition is particularly derelict.

No 5 ↑

3 & 5. Porchester Terrace
Bayswater
NO 3 ↑

18 Chesterfield Hill, Mayfair

MAYFAIR as a residential district of the highest pretensions suffered greatly in the 1920s and 1930s, when an increasingly hard pressed aristocracy tended to move out, or at least to retrench their way of life in the face of penal taxation, and commercial firms seeking a prestige address to move in. The wonder is that so much of Mayfair should still survive, but the erosion continues.

Peterborough had this justifiably critical paragraph to accompany my drawing:

"My Geoffrey Fletcher drawing illustrates a further—and particularly barbarous—stage in the destruction of Mayfair. The exquisite Georgian town house, No. 8, Chesterfield Hill, and No. 9 adjoining, are both to be razed and the site used as a car park. Something is clearly wrong, since neither house is listed as of architectural interest, though No. 8, with its unique projecting windows supported by elegant cast iron columns, is one of the best in the whole street."

Yet the house continues to survive, or did the last time I passed it— in an increasingly woebegone condition.

19 Gothic in Putney: The London Rowing Club

IT is a welcome relief once in a while to record changes that are on the side of the angels. Publishing this drawing in November, 1968, under the heading of *Keeping Up a Front*, Peterborough observed:

"Though their Putney Embankment clubhouse is 100 years old, the London Rowing Club's members voted unanimously last year against a plan to rebuild it completely. Under the new plan it will be thoroughly modernised inside, but the river front, with the long windows and balcony shown in Geoffrey Fletcher's sketch, will be preserved. Demolition work will be formally started by Graham Hill, the world champion racing driver, who is one of the club's 700 members. This will also mark the public launching of a £27,500 appeal for the modernisation. Its architect, Simon Crosse, is a former club oarsman, as was the building's designer, G. A. Dunnage, who rowed for the L.R.C. in the 1850s."

Even to the non-oarsman, there can be few places in London more satisfying than the long room of the club on a winter twilight, when the photographs of bearded oarsmen of long ago look from the walls at the dusky river, and firelight in a Gothic fireplace gives one a comforting sense of being cosily remote from the gathering mists of the chilly Thames.

52

20 From Contented Cows: Victorian mural panels, Crouch Hill

THE mural panel I illustrate, one of seven behind the United Dairies shop in Crouch Hill, on the Islington-Hornsey border, is a characteristic example of this increasingly rare type of Victorian decoration, usually found on shops and pubs.

All seven deal with dairying, and are carried out in incised cement infilled with Indian Red. The effect is heightened by the cut brick and stone façade of the former Friern Manor Dairy Farm which is their setting.

My drawing shows the panel *Present Day Delivery* in which a heavily-moustached milkman with his "pram" and 17-gallon churn delivers his wares in an idealised St. John's Wood setting of the late 1870s or early 1880s.

When the drawing was published, one of the directors of the Friern Manor Dairy Farm Ltd. wrote to tell me that fields surrounded the dairy when it was built in the last century, the cows at that time being milked on the premises.

BILL STICKERS WILL BE PROSECUTED

PRESENT DAY DELIVERY

21 Narrow Street, Limehouse

THIS is one of Peterborough's successful pleas for mercy: immediately after the publication of the drawing, the Stepney Borough Council decided the old houses should be preserved. Repair and restoration work by the individual owners is now going on. No such happy ending occurred with the old houses on the opposite shore in Rotherhithe, in one of which I lived. The L.C.C., despite powerful advocacy among the preservationists, demolished them.

Under the heading *Farewell to Limehouse*, the original paragraph accompanying this drawing read:

"The weakness of official 'protection' of ancient and historic buildings is illustrated by my Geoffrey Fletcher drawing of five early 18th-century buildings in Narrow Street, Limehouse, which the L.C.C. propose to demolish. Last of the old riverside houses of the East End, they are on the Ministry of Housing's supplementary list. Adjoining them is the Grapes pub, the original of Dickens's Six Jolly Fellowship Porters. Sea captains and sail makers used to live in this district and barge building was carried on until fairly recently. But now the L.C.C. say the houses' condition is too poor and their appearance of insufficient worth to justify preservation.

"In their stead we are promised an open space as 'a window on the river'. Not to mention another gap in London's history."

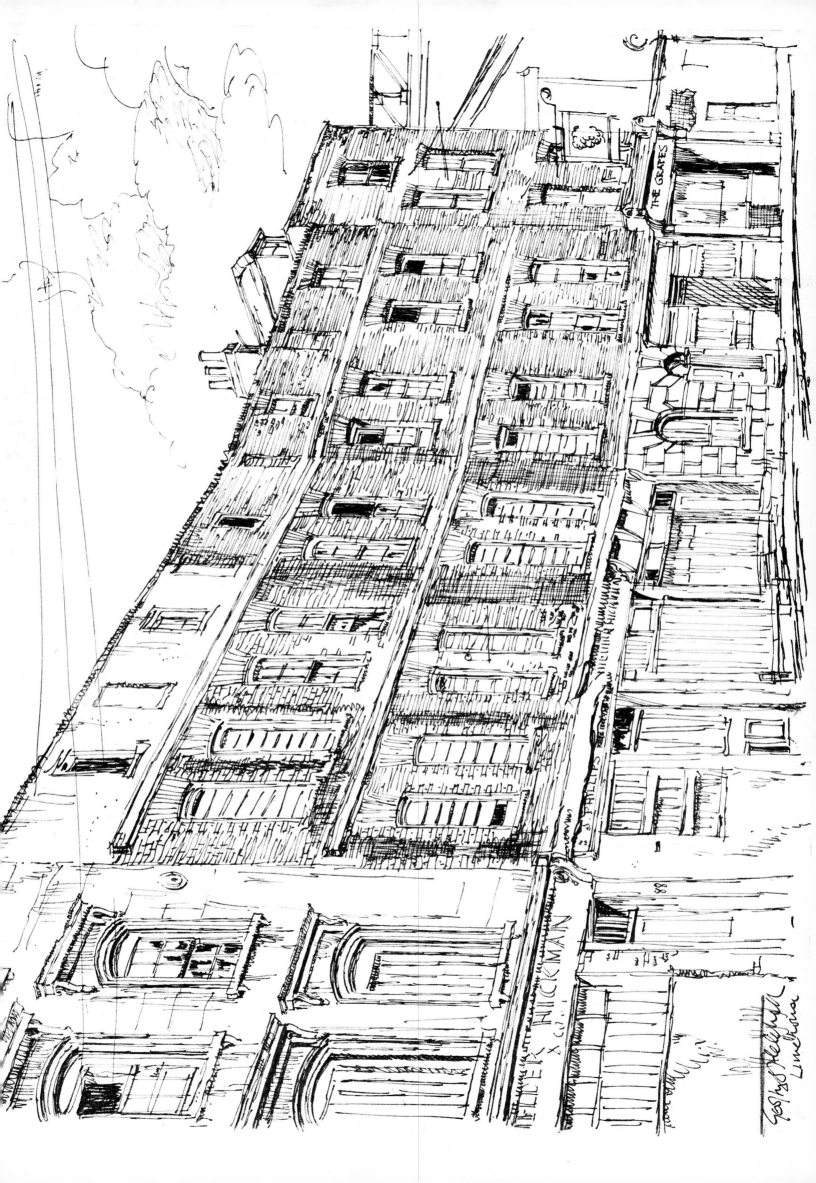

22 St. John the Divine, Kennington

MY drawing shows one of London's biggest churches, St. John the Divine in Kennington, whose crumbling stonework is causing concern.

Designed by Street, architect of the Law Courts, and dedicated in 1874, it represents him at his best. The impeccable proportions of the tower and spire and the quality of the detailing make this one of the most remarkable monuments of the Gothic Revival. St. John's was burnt out during the war and restored internally to its original pattern. But its fine Victorian carving is in over-soft Bath stone now becoming a potential danger to passers-by.

The G.L.C. has given £500 towards the £5,000 immediately needed for repairs.

The drawing was published in January, 1968.

23 The skyline of Westminster: A view from the bridge

THE heading for the paragraph accompanying this drawing when it was published in 1968 was *Another big blunder*. Peterborough remarked:

"My picture shows from Waterloo Bridge the damaging effect on the dignified proportions of the Westminster scene of the newest monstrosity—the 19-storey three-tower building rearing up in Marsham Street and Horseferry Road. It is destined in 1970 for Government departments—the Ministry of Housing will have the north and centre towers and about half the three-storey podium, and the Ministry of Transport the south tower and the other half of the podium.

"Big Ben and the Palace of Westminster, and the whole scene described as one of the finest in Europe, are put out of joint. Yet the curious thing is that, according to the Ministry of Public Building, the Royal Fine Art Commission and the planning authority approved the design. Models seem to prevent proper visualising. Anyone with imagination should have known how it would look from the river. The Government itself has pretty well destroyed the view of Westminster."

24 The Rape of Bloomsbury: Millman Street

THOSE who love Bloomsbury, as architecturally civilised a region as any capital city can show, had better take a last look at it before its unique character is finally eroded.

Rugby School failed in its assault on Great Ormond Street, but the larger part of four streets and a mews between there and Gray's Inn Road are now to be pulled down to make way for a G.L.C. school. My drawing shows a typical corner, Millman Place, which runs off Millman Street. London is thus losing more fine Georgian houses with many handsome details—doorways, staircases, railings and so on. They certainly needed attention but they need not have been allowed to deteriorate.

Perhaps the saddest part of this massacre is that it is being carried out in the name of education, the process begun years ago by London University farther to the west.

It was in Millman Street that that strange character, Charles Geneviève Louise Auguste André Timothée d'Eon de Beaumont— the Chevalier d'Eon—died in 1810. He was a French diplomatist and trusted agent of Louis XV. Having assumed women's dress on his first mission in Russia, he was required by his Government to continue wearing it. He did so for the rest of his life. . . . Bellingham also lodged in Millman Street when, in 1812, he assassinated Mr. Perceval in the lobby of the House of Commons.

25 Barnes Terrace

THE whole of London nowadays resembles nothing so much as a vast battlefield, with local engagements, hotly contested and nearly always against superior forces, flaring up all over the area at frequent intervals. In November, 1968, the following paragraph appeared with the drawing opposite:

"A vigorous fight is afoot in South West London against a plan to re-route the South Circular Road through the heart of an area house agents like to call Barnes's 'Little Chelsea'. Richmond Council justifies this on the quaint ground that the new route would follow the boundary between two parishes. The protestors, led by Mr. Paul Littleton, whose house is one of 80-odd that would be demolished, argue that it would destroy a village-style community and will in any case be made quite unnecessary by the G.L.C.'s London motorway plans. They also feel it will increase rather than diminish the traffic along Barnes Terrace, which contains some of London's finest Thames-side houses. The example in the drawing was once occupied by Gustav Holst, the composer."

On this, I can only comment that the colossal impertinence and the monstrous injustice of interfering—on the grounds of public utility— with the undeniable right of private individuals to enjoy their homes in peace is a tyranny quite beyond the confines of temperate language.

64

S&P Whitehall
Barnes Terrace Gustav Holst's House

26 A Tomb with a View

"ESPECIALLY after Francis Chichester's triumphant arrival," wrote Peterborough in December, 1966, "I was sad to hear that an earlier famous navigator, Captain Bligh of the *Bounty*, is being rather neglected. His tomb in St. Mary's churchyard, next to Lambeth Palace, is a handsome affair, as the drawing shows. At some time in the past, pieces of it have been restored in concrete. But now it looks extremely shabby and parts of the surrounding railings are missing. A little money would achieve a lot of restoration. Bligh, who died in 1817, lived at 100, Lambeth Road from 1794 to 1813. His tomb is next to that of the Tradescants, gardeners to Charles I, whose collections led to the founding of the Ashmolean Museum at Oxford."

I am glad to add as a postscript that Captain Bligh is no longer in eclipse. Shortly after the drawing appeared, the tomb was most carefully restored.

27 Former Parsonage of St. Margaret Pattens, Eastcheap

THE drawing appeared in May, 1968, with this paragraph:
"When the two 18th-century Eastcheap buildings in the centre of the drawing are pulled down shortly only the Regency shop on the left will remain of an attractive group including the church of St. Margaret Pattens.

"This part of the City has scarcely changed in 150 years and the demolition is deplorable. The corner shop is scheduled, but it would have been much better to leave the whole group intact. The Georgian buildings used to be St. Margaret's rectory, but no rector has lived there since the turn of the century, when this section of Eastcheap was known as Little Tower Street."

28 Whittington College, Highgate

"**I**F the Regency buildings I illustrate are pulled down," wrote Peterborough in December, 1962, "Londoners may as well concede victory to cars and lorries and resign themselves to a future of noise, smell and accidents. The place is Whittington College, Highgate, a group of almshouses designed about 1820 by George Smith for a charity founded by Dick Whittington. And it is not an irresponsible speculator who proposes to destroy it but the L.C.C. for a road 'improvement'. Local opinion is particularly incensed because, as Sir Albert Richardson assures me, the road could quite easily be re-routed further south, where the property involved is nondescript.

"The almshouses are one of the most attractive examples of early Gothic Revival left in London. . . . Our road planners have long been accused of putting machines first and civilised values nowhere. This latest example of what Sir Albert calls 'Moloch Avenue madness' suggests that the charge is only too accurate."

Of course, this charming group was demolished. I had thought that the aged inhabitants would have been distressed at their forcible uprooting and be attached to this sylvan spot. I found to my sorrow that the reverse was the case—that the only time they ceased to find fault with it was when they were complaining of the iniquities of their fellow inmates.

29 Riceyman Steps

T HE extensive demolitions now taking place along King's Cross Road between Vernon Rise and Great Percy Street are part of substantial changes overtaking Finsbury, until recently a district almost unchanged from the period when Arnold Bennett described it in his 1923 novel *Riceyman Steps*. The old shops in Gwynne Place (Granville Place in Bennett's day) have made way for a car park, but fortunately the stone steps themselves remain as a memorial to a vanished age. "Riceyman Square" (Granville Square) at the top of the steps has, however, been upgraded. Now repainted and restored, it no longer agrees with the novelist's description of it as decrepit and slatternly. The drawing was published in November, 1968.

Keejman Steps.

30 Brunswick House, Vauxhall

THIS drawing was published in September, 1968. The paragraph noted that this graceful late Georgian house, the only substantial survivor of the villas formerly on the edge of Vauxhall Gardens, is now a British Railways staff club. "But though safe at present," Peterborough continued, "it is not protected and it will be surrounded by the tall blocks of the new Covent Garden authority."

After publication, I had a very interesting letter from a *Daily Telegraph* reader of over 80, who told me that when she was a girl of twelve, she used to stay for weekends and go to Christmas parties at Brunswick House. A Mr. Richardson, brickmaker, occupied the place at that time, the firm's offices being also housed in the same building in the regular old London way. Most of the first floor was then a drawing room.

The semi-circular porch in the Adamesque manner is particularly fine.

Brunswick House
Vauxhall

31 Londonderry House, Park Lane

"NOTHING could be more symbolic of the changed pattern of London life than the present state of Londonderry House in Park Lane.

"At the turn of the century it was the setting for brilliant political receptions. Now it is to be demolished to make room for yet another 'luxury' hotel. This splendid mansion, of which my drawing shows the front, was built by Benjamin Wyatt about 1830 and the L.C.C. wanted it preserved. They were overruled, not for the first time, by the Ministry of Housing."

I well remember what a melancholy experience it was to go over the ruined house—a palace, rather. The great staircase, cracked and chipped, led to the salons above, dignified in their decay, though the gilded plaster was dropping from rich cornices and ugly gaps showed where fine mantelpieces had been torn out. There were strange whisperings in the empty rooms and corridors and shufflings that might well have been those of departed statesmen, still conniving and contriving though the game was over long ago.

Londonderry House
Park Lane

32 Charlie Chaplin's birthplace, Pownall Terrace, Kennington

CHARLIE CHAPLIN was born 80 years ago in the house that is the fifth arch from the right of the decayed Kennington group seen in the drawing and condemned to demolition when I drew it in 1964. The address is 3, Pownall Terrace.

It was quite a handsome place in a rural area when it was built at the turn of the nineteenth century. Today, few of the locals seem to know much about its distinguished former resident. However, a small girl was able to point out the birthplace to me. "But," she explained, "he doesn't live there any more."

Kennington, I might add, was a favourite place of residence for music hall artistes like Charlie Chaplin's father, being convenient for the various variety and music halls "on the Surrey side" of the water.

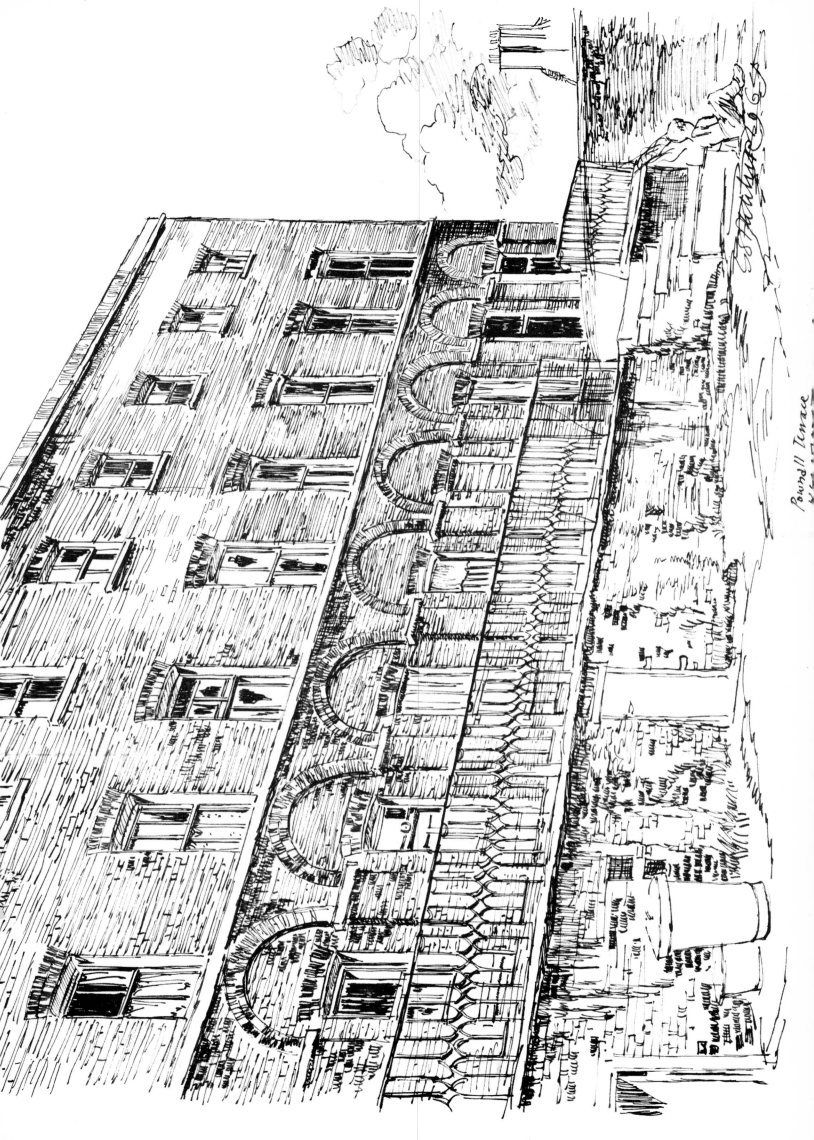

Burrell Terrace

33 Holy Trinity, Southwark

THE future of the disused Holy Trinity Church in Trinity Church Square, Southwark, remains undecided, despite discussions between the church authorities and the borough council. Both would like it preserved if a proper use for it is found.

It is a superb example of the Greek Revival, built in 1823 by Bedford, the architect of St. John's, Waterloo Road, in a part of London once much favoured by writers of popular songs. The church is said to be the one Tom Costello used to sing about—*At Trinity Church I Met My Doom*—a song written by a local resident, Fred Gilbert. In the square in front of the church is a medieval statue of a king said to have been rescued from the fire that destroyed the Houses of Parliament.

34 Duck Island, St. James's Park

OF all the houses-that-go-with-the-job in London, there is none, I believe, more delightful than the very desirable residence shown in my drawing. To live here in the heart of London, among wildlife and trees—not to mention the pelicans kept on the premises— yet within minutes of the life and movement of the great city, is surely the ultimate in human felicity.

This haven is the Victorian cottage orné on Duck Island in St. James's Park, built in 1840 by the Ornithological Society to the designs of their architect, F. B. Watson. The Treasury was generous enough to bear half the cost of this characteristic example of period picturesqueness.

In 1952 the house was found to be unsuitable for habitation and was condemned. But the Ministry of Works took it in hand, did a year's job of restoration, and very pretty the place looks as a result.

Duck Island

35   Carter Lane

THIS drawing was published in June, 1968, not long before the announcement of the plan which, if carried out, will destroy almost entirely the atmosphere and interest of the area. The publication of the drawing and paragraph below was followed by an unusual number of readers' protests, including one or two from architects.

"Another characteristic City corner—Carter Lane from the Blackfriars end—may not remain inviolate much longer. Beyond the attractive Georgian properties are a fine early 19th-century group and the unspoilt Wardrobe Place.

"But Carter Lane is in the middle of the Holford scheme coming shortly before the Court of Common Council. The idea is to keep 'whatever is worth saving'.

"That, however, is a vague phrase and many fear that this area, like too many others, will be dehumanised when the planners get to work on it."

36 Changing City skyline: The Bank and the new Stock Exchange

THE drawing, published in June, 1968, was accompanied by the following paragraph:

"The Bank of England is having its first clean since its pre-war reconstruction, a £20,000 job expected to take a year. My drawing shows the scene with the Royal Exchange on the right and, above the Bank, an intruder. This is the new 26-storey, 300 foot-high Stock Exchange going up in Throgmorton Street. It puts the whole architectural relationship out of joint."

These giant cereal packet blocks are at their most damaging in juxtaposition to the Wren churches, which, of course, were never intended to be seen against such Cyclopean backgrounds.

Geoffrey Fletcher 1968

37　Suffolk House, Laurence Pountney Hill

NO drawing of mine published in the *Daily Telegraph* during the last ten years has drawn more protests than this. Many of the letters and telephone calls expressing strong disapproval came from young office workers—those conventionally supposed to prefer the office blocks of the new up-to-the-minute London. Most, in fact, used the opportunity to work off their distaste for the de-humanising changes going on around them in the City. The most delightful comment was from an old lady who worked in Suffolk House as a girl and declared it to be "the finest office block ever designed by Sir Christopher Wren".

At the time of publication in June, 1968, the caption read:

"To judge from what happened when Geoffrey Fletcher was drawing for me the next unspoilt corner of the City to be broken up, London workers are becoming exasperated by the Corporation's willingness to sacrifice to redevelopment one attractive scene after another.

"This victim is Laurence Pountney Hill, off Cannon Street, an atmospheric assortment of Victorian Gothic offices and Georgian houses surrounding the parish churchyard. Suffolk House is an example of a 19th-century idiom of which the City has too little as it is.

"One passer-by after another expressed resentment to Mr. Fletcher at the impending destruction. Even young people said they preferred the present scene to the new blocks now punching holes all over the City—not because they are new but because they have so little character.

"Suffolk House occupies the site of the medieval Manor of the Rose, whose undercroft may be found during demolition."

F J Fletcher June 1968

Suffolk House

Laurence Pountney Hill

38 Rebuilding the Watch House, St. Sepulchre-without-Newgate

I ILLUSTRATE the final stages of rebuilding the Watch House of St. Sepulchre-without-Newgate, opposite the Old Bailey. This was built in 1791 to check the extensive snatching of bodies from the churchyard which was then much larger. The "resurrection men" raided it after the funerals and offered corpses for sale to the highest bidder at the Fortune of War Tavern on the corner of Cock Lane.

In 1941, the Watch House vanished in the blitz. The new one is among the most charming of the minor designs of Lord Mottistone's and Paul Paget's architectural partnership.

Seen on the wall in the drawing is the Lamb memorial from Christ Church, Greyfriars, which is not being rebuilt. Another fine item from it, an iron gate, is to be erected soon.

The Watch House provides a new parsonage house with a choir vestry behind. It will also be useful should body snatching break out again.

39 Et Praeterita Nihil

MY Bloomsbury drawing of Millman Street (No. 24) shows handsome Georgian houses which are involved in a wholesale destruction to make room for a new school. This one illustrates an example of social as well as architectural vandalism in the same region.

No. 54 Hunter Street, part of a terrace in sound condition, was Ruskin's birthplace in 1819. A hotel for many years and now empty, it has survived almost unchanged. He describes his childhood there in *Praeterita*, his charming fragment of autobiography. What interested him most was to watch the water-carts being filled from the stand-pipe in the street outside.

The house is now caught up in the Foundling Estate rebuilding scheme, which will be largely residential—a fact that makes the destruction even less justified.

In view of the influence Ruskin's economic and social writings had on the wearing out of industrial injustice, class hatred and greed, it is especially sad that in the year of the 150th anniversary of his birth, 1969, Englishmen will allow this, the last of his London homes, to disappear. What this part of Bloomsbury is going to get in place of eighteenth-century refinement is something roughly resembling a huge football stadium.

Ruskins birthplace
54 Hunter St
Brunswick Sq

54

RUSKIN HOUSE

Schrytt Mitchell 1968

54 Hunter Street
Brunswick Square

40   An old flame: The sewer gas ventilating lamp in the Savoy

THIS drawing published in 1968 had the following note:
"Many of the 50-year-old gas lamp standards are vanishing from streets and alleys off the Strand as Westminster Corporation pursues its aim of total conversion to electricity. But I hope the one Geoffrey Fletcher has drawn for me will escape this passion for standardisation.

"It is the beautiful sewer-gas destructor lamp in Carting Lane, at the side of the Savoy Hotel. Now the only one left in London, it has been for many years drawing up vapours from below ground by means of its four gas burners and lighting the street as well.

"Electrification would ruin both its function and its interest."

Always a believer in gas lighting as opposed to electricity, I am glad to be able to add, as a postscript, that so many Londoners have written to the Westminster Council pleading for the lamp that the authorities have decided to preserve it, running it as hitherto on town gas, as a curiosity.

Savoy